Manhattan

Ned Swan

Copyright Ned Swan 2016. All rights reserved.

ISBN 978-194560354-9

These poems art dedicated to everyone in New York City that I touched, and who touched me.

Table of contents

Manhattan Lullaby 1
Bradley's is Gone 36
The Gym 39
Toe to Toe 52
Snow 58
What Happened Bill? 64
One Starry Night in Brooklyn 68
The Music King 76

Manhattan Lullaby

Prologue

New York burned me

Like a laser

All those memories

All those dreams

Lifetimes up and passed

Burned on my gut

With a merciless heat

Scarred over

And re-burned again

So deep

So sharp

So vivid

I left

Years ago

But I read

The Empire Diner

Had closed

And the owner,

Jack Doenias, is dead

And that brought

Everything rushing back

Someone said

That they loved my poems

Because reading them

Was like seeing yourself

Through the experience of another

But all those memories

I have of New York

I no longer know the person

That lived them

It's like seeing

My past

Through the experiences

Of another

A film that's vaguely familiar

But fiction

Part 1

I remember the 1970's

Living in Chelsea

It was gritty and cheap

Puerto Rican bodegas

On Eighth Avenue

Above 14th Street

Filling, cheap, and tasty

Cuban/Chinese meals

At Mi Chinita diner

Or the little green painted Asia di Cuba

When I learned that 25 years later

An expensive, fashionable eatery

In the painfully trendy St. Martin's Hotel

Opened under the name, Asia di Cuba

I nearly puked in disgust

In Chelsea of those days

No galleries

No fashionable hotels

Just dumps

Where alcoholics on welfare crashed

Warehouses

Longshoremen's unions

Irish waterfront beer joints

And some lovely 19th century

Brick, row houses

That families

Of relatively modest means

Could buy

In this distinctly

Unfashionable

District

The abandoned West Side Highway

Traced the Hudson shore

Broken Tarmac grown through

With persistent weeds and grass

Dangerous holes in the surface

Covered over with rusting squares

Of corrugated iron sheeting

It was forbidden to go there

But we used it to run

From 15th Street

Almost to the Battery

And back

How we could run

In those days!

Every Sunday

I would stop at my friend's

Apartment on the Upper West Side

Near Central Park

And we ran

The six mile circuit

Around the Park

Sprinting a race the last

Half mile

But I could never

Beat my friend

It didn't even make us tired

Sometimes we'd head over

To a playground

On Columbus Avenue

For a couple of hours

Of basketball

In the hot afternoon

We were ludicrously fit

Thinking back

About it now

I can barely believe it

We all played basketball

Football and softball

In the Lawyers Leagues

In addition to working

Absurdly long hours

As junior lawyers

(think, serfs)

In New York

Law practices

1976

The Celebration of 200 American

Years

Watching the Tall Ships procession

From the balcony

Of a tower block

High above

The Hudson River

On a bright summer's day

A friend of Polish descent

Shouting

"Polska, Polska"

As the big, square rigger

From Poland

Floated by

Pushed by

The brisk summer wind

I became a lawyer

That year

I was so young

You have heard the expression

"Will work for food"?

Well, I did.

In 1977

I left the law firm

Where I had worked

For 2 years

To set up my own practice

With no clients

Little money

And a great view

From a little office

High in Rockefeller Center

At a rent

I had no way to pay

Every day,

I dressed in my

Brooks Brothers suit

Took my brief case

Tap-danced

Past the bronze statue

Of Atlas into my office

Well, in my romantic

Imagination

In reality

I can't tap dance

And read

The New York Times

Every page

Every story

Every day

After a couple of weeks

I started to get referrals

From friends, classmates,

Acquaintances

Of people

Who needed legal help

But couldn't pay much

All kinds of matters

All kinds of people

So I paid the rent

And learned

That world was

A very strange place

There was

The successful

Commercial artist

Who lived with

The composer

Who was so shy and retiring

He could never invite

Her to his concerts

Or even play the piano

In her presence

And could only

Occasionally

Let her hear parts

Of the recordings

Of his composition

Of course

He never composed a note

Played her pieces of

Ralph Vaughn William's recordings

Couldn't play

The formidable grand piano

She bought for him

And ran off with all her money

But that's just

One more New York story

There was the contract

Negotiation

With a representative

Of the Teamster's Union

He was built like

A walking refrigerator

Big gold chain

Around his neck

That was set off by

By a jagged scar

Across his throat

And face

"I don't want no trouble, Kid."

Was his jocular opening line

To which my

Silent

Rejoinder, was

"That's Mr. Kid,

"To you, Pal."

Let's not forget

The contract

Signed in a room

At the Plaza Hotel

Witnessed by two

Call girls

In which the feckless

Playboy son

Of an immensely rich

South American industrialist

Promised his family would pay

Millions to two dodgy characters

For services his father

Did not need

Sometimes I got

To sue powerful

International conglomerates

Once an old and sophisticated

European consultant

Put his arm around my shoulders

In Paris

In the midst of such a case

He said,

"Twenty years ago, you'd be dead"

"But things are different now."

How different? I thought.

But back to food

One client was the exuberant

Owner of a small luxury deli

On Hudson street

He paid me in food

Exotic, imported food

Such as I had never even

Dreamed about before

Cheeses, charcuterie, pastries

It was all a revelation

I happily worked for food

Then my daughter was born

At Roosevelt Hospital

A lovely little thing

But terrifying

How could I support her?

I was such a small fish

In the sea of New York lawyers

Eating my lunch

In an Irish bar

In Hell's Kitchen

The day after she was born

Life seemed so uncertain

But I would try

Leafy West 21st street

With the Seminary across the street

Clement Clark Moore taught Greek there

When he wasn't writing

"A Visit from St. Nicholas"

Or, "The Night Before Christmas"

As it is often known

We had a lovely garden,

And a first floor apartment there

In an old fashioned brownstone

Owned by a writer lady

One of the buildings

Built by Rev. Moore

When he developed his family's

Manhattan farm

Into the grid of streets and homes

That became Chelsea

Tony Perkins was a neighbor

That made you think twice

About taking a shower

But he seemed nice enough

No sign of Norman Bates

Living with his new beautiful wife

Berry Berenson

She's dead now, of course

One of the many tragic

Airplane victims

Of the 9/11 atrocity

But I remember the day

In the late 1970's

When Jack and his partners

Opened the Empire Diner

A monument to Chelsea's transformation

To cool

And a landmark in my life

Tony Perkins stood in the midst

Of the crowded, sunny diner

In baseball cap, and a big smile

Holding his new baby in his arms

With his wife at his side

My wife and I would bring our baby in

To the Empire Diner

Lay her on the table

While we ate,

And Jack would make kind remarks

About how beautiful and well-behaved

She was

Years later, when I had moved to London

And the Empire Diner was no longer

On the other side of my garden wall

I went there one night

For memory's sake

Jack, was,

As he was so often

Sitting at the counter

I showed him a picture

Of the beautiful 18 year old

My daughter had grown into

He was taken aback by the passage

Of so much time

An Empire Diner baby

Had become a woman

And now he's gone

And my daughter is 35

Still beautiful

Perhaps not quite so well-behaved

What would Jack say now?

The Bethesda Fountain

Why does that remain

So vivid in my memory?

Off the 72d Street

Central Park crossing

Is it because I saw

My first ever rollerbladers there

It was 1972

How unusual,

I thought

I passed John and Yoko

Walking through the Park

Near there

One bright summer's day

They walked briskly

Arms around

Each other's waists

Acknowledging

Us civilians

With steady smiles

John's hair was cropped

Quite short then

Almost shaved

They lived nearby

At 72d Street

On Central Park West

In the fantastical Dakota

Up 'til then

Famous as the setting

For "Rosemary's Baby"

I did not then imagine

That the city

John had come

To love so well

Would kill him so brutally

After that terrible murder

A friend of mine

An able Harvard Law Graduate

Was appointed by the Court

To represent John's killer

He had to move out

Of his apartment

Because of death threats

But

He was un-intimidated

And, although I doubt

It gave him any personal pleasure

He carried out his duties

Calmly and professionally

Remembering Central Park

I always think

Of Her

The dark-haired, curvaceous

Young beauty that I used take there

I was shocked when

She told me she wanted me

From the first time

She saw me walk by

She was young

Terribly bright

And ferociously ambitious

She lived in a tiny room

In a YMCA

No private bathroom

But that didn't stop

Us from impassioned

Love-making

On many hot

Summer afternoons

I knew I was just

Another one

Of her youthful

Exploratory adventures

But I was no less

Grateful

For that

Part 2

I can't forget

Those hot, hot

Manhattan August days

When you stagger

From air-conditioned building

To air-conditioned building

In the lightest weight summer suits

You could buy

On those days

You didn't want wool

Anywhere near

Your sticky, grimy skin

The extremes were so great

On a summer Saturday

If you went to the movies

You had to wear shorts, a T-shirt and sandals

To survive the summer heat

When travelling there

But inside the cinema

The air conditioning

Was so cold

They could have stored meat

What were we doing

Playing competitive squash

In hundred degree heat?

But there was a summer league

When we played

The Heights Casino Club

In Brooklyn

Their stuffy

Unairconditioned courts

Were so hot

You had to win

In three straight games

If the match went to five

You were dead

We were young and stupid

Begging for heart attacks

And we were lawyers and doctors

Who had studied at Harvard

If anyone had died

I suppose the lawyers

Would have sued

The doctors

For negligently failing

To advise us properly

Hey! What do you want?

We were New York lawyers

The doctors would have

Expected us to sue them

That's why they have insurance

Part 3

Chelsea was my part

Of New York

In those days

A faded

Poor part of Manhattan

Squeezed in

Between

The Meat-Packing district

And Hell's Kitchen

Chelsea then was so gritty

Down at the heels

And unglamorous

They used to film "Kojack" there

It was the capital of New York Punk

The rundown, black-painted

Elgin Cinema

Sat in the middle of 8th Avenue

Offering unknown bands

Like The New York Dolls,

And somebody called Blondie

Never saw them

I couldn't afford to go

I used to walk by the Chelsea Hotel

Almost every day

To me

A most holy temple

A Pantheon to the gods of art

Dylan Thomas lived there

While he drank himself

To death at the White Horse Tavern

On Hudson Street

Arthur Miller lived there

When he wrote

"Death of a Salesman"

It's where Bob Dylan wrote

"Sad Eye Lady of the Lowlands"

Where Andy Warhol made

"Chelsea Girls"

And where

Sid Vicious murdered

Poor Nancy Spungeon

There is no place

On earth

More consecrated

To the creativity

And insanity

Of the arts

So

When I needed

A place to live

It had to be there

On 23rd Street

Between 7th and 8th Avenues

Because is it not obvious

That I too

Am a great artist

Or,

If I am not now

That I inevitably will be?

Never mind

I had to go there

To negotiate for a room

With Mr. Bard

The Chelsea's

Charming

Talkative and

Art loving owner

In his tiny ground floor office

Surrounded by poorly curated

Early paintings

Worth a damn fortune

By Andy Warhol,

And other famous artists

He hosted at their beginnings

"We're competing with

The Plaza here"

He proudly told me

Not as a hotel

I thought

Because the Chelsea

Was not five-star

Bedroom collection

It was a an atmosphere

A monument

A mausoleum

A dream

A ghost

An inspiration

The actual rooms are better

Left to the imagination

And the cockroaches

Who are the prime tenants

But I absolutely loved

Living in the Chelsea Hotel

In the creaking

Old-fashioned elevator

I frequently met

Virgil Thompson

The composer

Of the beautiful symphonic tributes

To the settlers

Of the American West

"The Plough that Broke the Plains"

And "The River"

Both written for

FDR's government-supported

Arts project

The Works Progress Administration

The WPA

But New York

Was just full of dreams

And reminiscences

That I borrowed

For myself

The first few years

I lived there

Every day I had

To walk from our

Little basement flat

In Chelsea

To Washington Square

Where the Law School was

I lived on 15th Street

On the edge of

The Meatpacking District

But crossing 14th Street

Was like passing through

An enchanted door

Because now I was

In Greenwich Village

The fabled font

Of art, music, poetry, drama

Ideas, protest, revolution, politics

Education, coffee houses

And Italian food

To a boy, recently living

In rural New Hampshire

The intensity

And richness of the experience

Overwhelmed

Every one of my senses

The shortest route

Was down Greenwich Avenue

First, past the corner

Immortalized

In Edward Hopper's

Iconic coffee shop painting

"Nighthawks"

Then past

The Village Vanguard

Where they played

The greatest jazz

In the history of the world

Where the Bill Evans

Took piano playing

To galaxies previously

Unknown

Before drink and drugs

Stiffened his fingers forever

For that reason alone

I have no forgiveness

For drink and drugs

Crossing 7th Avenue

Passing St. Vincent's Hospital

Where Dylan Thomas

Breathed his last

And where the front line was

Where they fought the losing battle

Against the plague of AIDs

In the mid-1980s

That wiped out Christopher Street

Making it a parade of ghosts

And where they would later

Treat me for nearly fatal

Head injuries

Suffered in an ill-advised

Street fight

With five guys

I took a dislike to

Then past the Peacock Cafe

The Village's first

Italian coffee shop

A supplier of good coffee

And decent inexpensive

Italian dishes

I loved their veal pizziola

On lower Greenwich Avenue

Next to where

The Women's House of Detention

Used to stand

Behind the

New York High School

For the Performing Arts

Of "Fame" fame

One the odd things about

The Peacock was

The 8 foot tall bronze statue

Of a goat-eared Pan

Standing on a globe

While playing his pipes

It took up a huge amount

Of space

In the middle of this little coffee shop

You could hardly squeeze by it

To get to your table

Of to the coffee counter

One day a research assistant

Walked into the Peacock

And nearly fainted from shock

The Pan was a lost work

By a famous 19th century sculptor

The art world

Had been searching for it

For decades

Today, it occupies the center

Of the entrance

To the American Wing

Of the Met

On indefinite loan

From the long-vanished

Peacock Cafe

Walk just past there

And you are walking past

Patchin Place

Where ee cummings lived.

You are on

Avenue of the Americas now

At Greenwich Village Square

It's one of those places

Where if you stood there

Long enough

Every person

You ever knew

Or ever heard of

Would pass by

Just ahead of you

Bo Diddley

Is crossing the street

In dark shades, and

His trademark

Black Homburg hat

Wasn't it the

Rolling Stones

Who sang the lyric

"Bo Diddley, Bo Didley"

"Where'd you go?"

Well, I could have told them

On the other side of the Avenue

Richard Gere is coming

Out of Balduccis

With 2 heavy shopping bags

And a smile for everyone

As he headed back to his apartment

On 8th Street

Balducci's had

It's buffula mozzarella

Flown in fresh every day

From Sicily

Rumor had it that

This was not its

Only connection with Sicily

Which I guess is why

In the film

"Married to the Mob"

The head gangster is shown

Generously bringing groceries

To his girlfriend

In two big

Balducci's shopping bags

But now Balducci's

Like the Empire Diner

Is gone

A ghost

In the broken hearted memories

Of its Greenwich Village devotees

Part 4

I left Manhattan years ago

But I can still dream now of

Long lost local apparitions

Such as the Fairy of Greenwich Village

Who would appear late at night

Wearing a long, full-skirted, white formal, dress,

A sparkling tiara, and holding

A star-tipped wand

As he glided and pirouetted

On old fashioned, four-wheeled,

White-booted roller skates

In the vicinity of the northern intersection

Of Greenwich and Seventh Avenues

Or the Purple People

Who flashed about

Village on their purple bikes

In matching

Psychedelicly tie- dyed

Purple outfits

And purple flat caps

He, of scraggly beard

Round, steel-rimned

Purple-tinted spectacles

And long, unkempt

Greying hair

She, much younger

Surprisingly pretty

With long sandy blonde hair

And her own purple spectacles

Always energetically peddling

A respectable distance behind

The Purple Man

Where are they now?

This poem is already too long

A futile attempt

To tie up in a few careful words

And struggling stanzas

The blinding constellation

Of feelings

Experiences

Sights and sounds

Lights

Buildings

Shops

Snow

Ice

Food

People

Music

Fears

Joys

Sex

The rivers

The sea

The courts

The police

The classrooms

And the parks

That I with

My limits

My prejudices

My tunnel vision

My narrow experiences

And my short life

Can only begin

To describe

But really

I did this

Only to find out

One thing

Manhattan,

If I ever came back

Could you love me

Now

As I loved you then?

Bradley's is Gone

Bradley's is gone now

For two years

I lived in the East Village

On 11th Street

Between 5th Ave

And University Place

Around the corner

From Bradley's

Bradley Cunningham's

Atmospheric

15 table club

For great and journeyman

Jazz musicians

Paul Desmond, Charles Mingus,

Thelonious Monk, Kenny Barron

And enough others to write

A history of jazz about

Spent their time there

It was great to go there

At night

Order some of their good food

And a beer

And listen to some fine

Piano and bass duets

But for me

Bradley's proximity

Made it more

Than an occasional club

Where I heard some good music

By day it was a friendly refuge

Always welcoming

Where you could get a good meal

And relax

I remember one Thanksgiving

Emergency session

Where my wife was too

Sick with flu to cook,

Or even eat

The traditional holiday meal

To give her some peace

In our small apartment

My daughter and I

Went over to Bradley's

To eat a nice Thanksgiving

Turkey dinner there

The staff was really kind

It could not have been

A more perfect home

Away from home

Bradley Cunningham

Died some years ago

Bradley's closed

But the musicians

And ordinary

Neighborhood denizens

Like myself

Hold on to our

Fond syncopated memories

Thank you Kenny Barron

For those two recorded tributes

"Live at Bradley's" I and II

(Sunnyside Records)

One part of the second

Recording

Kenny titled "The Perfect Set"

It fits

In my memory

Bradley's was

The Perfect Set

The Gym

The scariest thing

About

Gleason's Gym

Was the shower

Not for Police reasons

For

Board of Health

Reasons

Only

Boxing

In a full sweatsuit

T-shirt

Shorts

Helmet

Gloves

Handwraps

And tape

In the hundred degree

Sauna

Of a Midtown

Manhattan

Summer

Could get you

In there

To take

A shower

Rocky Davis

Always

Wore dark sunglasses

In the Gym

At night

He was my trainer

Twelve dollars an hour

But no

Fooling around

I had to be

Serious

He had his pros

To train

Like

The great

Mike McCallum

"The Body Snatcher"

Three time

Three weight

World Champion

I went

Night after night

Trying to learn

The footwork

How to jump rope

How to move

And then

How to punch

How to hit

A bag

Without

Breaking

Your wrist

How to

Step

Into a punch

How to

Snap it

How to

Avoid a punch

How to

Hold your hands

Up

To protect

Yourself

Crucial

If your hands fell

So would you

Repetition

Repetition

Sweating

Buckets

Three rounds

Moving in the ring

Jumping rope

An art in itself

Three minutes on

One minute off

Working the bags

Three minutes on

One minute off

By the bells

Sit-ups

Pushups

By the bells

Everything

By the bells

Finally, learning to spar

Going up against other fighters

In the ring

One round

Then two

Three

Four

Five

And then six

You have no idea

How exhausting that is

Until you have done it

That is why

I think

They should take

Every fat

Alcohol sodden

Fag sucking

Sportswriter

Who ever called

A professional fighter

A "bum"

And make him

Try ten rounds

With a ordinary

Journeyman fighter

Then

They might finally

Begin to understand

What it takes

To stand up

In that ring

For thirty minutes

How many miles you have to run

How many sit-ups you have to do

How many hours you have to work those bags

How may rounds you have to spar

How many months you need to train

Just to keep your left hand

Raised high enough to

Protect your chin

While your head

Your face and

Your body

Are absorbing

The powerful punches

Of a professional boxer

Knowing that

If your left hand

Drops

Just a few inches

From fatigue

Or pain

You

Are going to get hit

With a right hook

That will knock you out

End your career

Make you a vegetable

Or kill you

No professional fighter

Deserves the insults

The cynical media

Think clever or

Amusing

Every one

Has earned

The common decency

Of our respect

For his discipline

His determination

His courage

And his hope

One I saw there regularly

Was Gerry Cooney

Gerry was 6'6" tall

And outweighed me

By 40 pounds

He had 28 professional fights

Winning 24

By knockouts

"Ring Magazine"

Rated him 53

On their list of the

"100 Greatest Punchers of All Time"

When I met him

He was the

World Number One

Heavyweight Contender

His previous fight

Had been against Larry Holmes

For the

World Heavyweight Championship

That night in Las Vegas

Cooney's payday had been

Ten Million Dollars

But Holmes won

In the 13th Round

In the summer of 1984

Gerry was training for

His fight against Phillip Brown

Who he would

Knockout

In the 5th round

In September

One hot August night

Before then

Rocky said to me

Victor Valle

(Gerry's trainer)

Asked if you

Would go a few rounds

With Gerry

OK

I said

But don't

Fool around with him

This is for real

OK

I understand

Before we started

Gerry showed his

Disdain for me

By refusing to wear

His mouthguard

Who was I?

I wasn't

Gonna hit him

The bell rang

I hit him in the face

With two quick jabs

He stopped

And had

His mouthguard

Put in

We traded punches

But I got mine in

And was holding my own

He was bigger

But I was quicker

The second round

His size began to matter

I was hitting him

But the weight

Of his punches

Was beginning

To get to me

Between rounds

Rocky asked me

"How are you doing?"

"I don't know, Rocky,

He's hitting me pretty good."

"Yeah,

"But you're taking it

"Beautiful"

Was his

Encouraging reply

The bell rang

Gerry broke

My nose

I defended myself

And hit back

Pretty well

But I knew the third

Was my last round

At the final bell

I came out

To the congratulations

Of the trainers

And the fighters

Rocky beamed

With pride

Saying,

"When I met him,

"He couldn't even walk!"

After we'd changed

"Gentleman Gerry"

Stopped me

And shook my hand

"I'm sorry about your nose."

"It's O.K."

"You've got a good jab."

"Thanks."

Rocky died

Of a heart attack

Not long after

I stopped going

To the Gym

But the sights

The sounds

The smells

And the people

There

Are burned into

My memory

For life

Toe to Toe

I was at the Royal Academy

Viewing an exhibition

Of contemporary

American

Artists

When I noticed

That the man

Standing

Next to me

Was David Bowie

Looking

Young

And fabulous

With a big smile

For everyone

Who recognized him

While he admired

A painting

By the American

Abstract expressionist

Frank Stella

Another time

I was at

The Art Institute of Chicago

In front of

Another work

By Frank Stella

Where a guide

Was explaining

To a large

Group of tourists

The importance

Of this collection

Of monochromatic

Striped quadrangles

With the incomprehensible

Spanish title

"De la nada vida a la nada muerte"

"From life nothing to death nothing"

One both occasions
I secretly smiled

Remembering the time
When I was
A serious competitor

To the Great
Frank Stella

I used to
Play squash

As Captain
Of the D Team
Of the Harvard Club
Of New York City

One hot summer night

Our scheduled opponent
Was
Park Place Squash Club

Not far
From the TriBeCa
Art hatchery

Before my game
I stood contemplating
The odd angles
Presented by
The squash court
Of their basement clubhouse

When
In came my opponent

Squash fanatic
Frank Stella

We sized each other up
Across
Centuries of art history

I immediately realized
That the unconventional
Construction of the court
Offered
A significant advantage
To an abstract expressionist

Nevertheless
I was determined
Not to be intimidated

By his mastery
Color and form

His integration
Of the influences
Of
Caravaggio
And Melville

Or sales of his
Paintings
At 4 million dollars

Each

But although

The New York

Art critic

Hilton Kramer

Called Stella's work

"The worst and silliest

"I have seen

"In nearly fifty years

"Of reviewing exhibitions"

He beat me

And worse

His art outsells mine

By a colossal margin

Snow

Snow

Blanketing

The late-night the streets

How beautiful

A child of the North

Snow was always

For me

A protective blanket

That, when young

Shielded me

From a world

I did not understand

And now old

Raises memories

Of happy times

A small boy

I stood by

The night window

Of my room

Looking

Into the streetlight's

Stream of electrons

Trying to gauge

The intensity

Of the snowfall

Would there

Be enough inches

To shield me

From the brain-freezing boredom

Of school?

That would only

Be settled the next day

Standing next to the radio

Listening hopefully

To the rapid-fire reading

Of the list of Central Massachusetts

Towns

That cancelled school that day

"Auburn"

Freedom!

To slide down

The unsanded side

Of Windsor Avenue

Throw snowballs

And set off

On frozen journeys

Through the snowy Siberia

Of boyhood imagination

Later,

Adolescents

My brother and I

Would accompany

My grandfather

To his snowbound house

On Lake Winnipesaukee

We chopped holes

In the ice

To carry buckets of water

Up to the house

Ate my grandfather's

Beaver tail stew

And lay in bed at night

Next to the black and silver

Wood burning stove

Listening to

The deep base booming

Of the expanding splitting ice

By day I skated on the lake

Coat sailing for miles

Across the glassy surface

While my grandfather and brother

Ice-fished in the hut

Gramp had hauled on to the ice

Every winter

Two days a week

My grandfather would take

My brother and I

To be first on the chairlift

At Gunstock mountain

Where we skied until

The mountain closed

And our legs felt like rubber

A young man

I reveled in the rare

Blizzards of New York

For the brief

Opportunity

They gave me

To recall

The white magic

Of my youth

One day I walked

Out of my tiny

Basement room

In the Meatpacking District

The business of which

In those days

Was meat

Into the teeth of a glorious

Blizzard

Joyfully walking all the way

Up Fifth Avenue

Exulting

In the pale solitude of

The thick white blanket

Imposed on the city

Near the Steuben Glass Building

My lonely journey was interrupted

By a lone figure

Slowly progressing

Towards me

Through a heavy veil

Of descending snowflakes

In a broad-brimmed

Black hat

A full length

Grey fox-fur coat

With a long

Silver-headed

Black walking stick

As he passed me

It appeared that

I did not exist

For him

And perhaps I didn't

Because when

I recognized

His dramatic

Black moustaches

I felt in the presence

Of an experience

More magically

Surreal

Than any work

By

Salvador Dali

What Happened Bill?

Weren't Gloria's steps

Enough to keep you

With us

Music genius

Is not about

How you dress

Where you come from

Your education

What you drink

What you smoke

Or what you inject

It's about what you feel

What you see

The movie playing

In your head

And

How effectively

You can communicate it

No one was better than you

Hey, man

There are radio stations

In Japan

That play nothing

But Bill Evans!

Sometimes, I feel like those radio stations

Some days

You are all I want to hear.

When Kind of Blue

Was being cut

Someone asked,

"What's the white boy doing here?"

Miles said,

"He's here because

He can play."

How you could play!

Sunday afternoons

At the Village Vanguard

On 7th Avenue

Your trio

You leading on the piano

Beautiful

Impressionistic

Bebop

Emotions

Cut to the bone

Lightly sketched scenes

The dreams

Of the audience

To fill in the gaps

You were the Matisse

The Seurat

The Picasso

Of Jazz

I know that

When Scott La Faro died

In that car crash

It hit you hard

His bass was so tight

But he was not

The making of you

He complimented you

Beautifully

But you were your own man

It was what was born in you

That made that music

You did not need that heroin

It was a deadly affectation

When I hear those keys

Signaling those elusive chords

That perfect timing

I think of what might have been

If only

You would have stayed with us

One Starry Night in Brooklyn

I remember sitting in a cinema

In New York

Looking up at the screen

Transfixed

By the beauty

Of the young woman

Playing Tom Conti's

Muse

In some forgettable

Suburban romance

And thinking

Is she real?

Can beauty so magical

Inhabit my world?

Brooklyn

Was a lonely place

It was a sharp

Cold winter

And I was living alone

In a bare flat

Near Prospect Park

Too far

From the bright life

Of Manhattan

I found

What comfort

I could

In the modest stimulation

Of taking my evening meals

In the limited selection

Of neighborhood restaurants

One was McFeely's

An artificially jovial

Irish-themed pub

With passable food

When I went there

On this night

It was almost empty

But as I chose a table

In the dining area

My spirits were lifted

To see a beautiful

Young woman

Sitting alone

Reading Pirandello

Summoning

More courage

Than I have ever had

Before

I spoke to her

And suggested

That since

We were both

Eating alone

Wouldn't it be

A good idea

If I joined her

To enhance our dinner

With pleasant conversation?

Amazingly

She agreed

I lost myself

In her sapphire eyes

The delicate features of

Her lovely face

Her honey colored hair

And her, long

Glorious figure

As we talked about

Her studies at

The Julliard School

Being on the cover

Of Vogue

Her friendship

With Mick Jagger

And how

Harrison Ford

Had not

Been very nice

To her

Subjects

I didn't usually

Cover

It was getting late

The restaurant

Was starting to close

Would I like

To come back to

Her apartment

And watch a

John Sayles film

With her?

She asked

I have always

Been

A big fan

Of

John Sayles

As we walked

Along

The wintery

Brooklyn streets

She said to me,

"You must have

Loads of women

After you

All the time."

I don't remember

What I replied

But I certainly thought

"Not so many

As you would think"

We watched part

Of the film

Talked of her

Disappointments

In love

The problems of

Being a single woman

In New York

And shared kisses

And embraces

Then

It was time for me

To go

We arranged to meet

Next Saturday

She wrote out

Her contact details

On a slip of paper

One last parting kiss

And I was back out

On the cold, quiet

Brooklyn street

Then it clicked

She was the girl

That magical girl

I had seen

On that cinema screen

Those months before

And I had

Held her

In my arms

For real

Tightly clasping

The slip of paper

She had given me

I floated effortlessly

Back

On the icy air

To my empty

Brooklyn

Apartment

That Thursday

Her new film

Was released

By Friday

She was so famous

We never

Spoke again

So

When she got

Her Oscar nomination

I was not with her

On

The Red Carpet

The Music King

On 10th July 1985

I was on a overnight flight

From London to New York

You know how it is

Seven hours

You try to sleep

You try to read

You don't say a word

To the person next to you

But as we came in to land

The guy next to me

Began to talk to me

He was from Birmingham

It was his first ever

Trip to New York

He managed a band

That had done a musical

Called "Chess"

He had some business

In New York

In connection with that

He did not know

A soul in the City

Could I recommend

Anything to do

I gave him my card

"Call me", I said,

"We'll do something."

When he did call the next day.

I felt at a bit of a loss.

I lived and worked

In the City

But I was not exactly

Mr. Party Guy

I didn't know much

About the nightlife

So I bought a copy

Of The Village Voice

The arbiter

Of all things "hip"

In New York

There, I found a notice

That Lonnie Mack

Was appearing

At the Lone Star Cafe

In the Village

Not far from where I lived

I had never heard

Of Lonnie Mack

But the Voice said

He was a well-respected guitarist

With couple minor hits

The Lone Star Cafe

Was a small, grungy blues, rock and country bar

On 5th Avenue and 13th St.

With passable bar food

And a giant statue

Of an Iguana

On the roof

Worth a try

I thought

Bound be to a contrast

From Birmingham

We met there

Ordered our beers and burgers

And listened to Lonnie play

His better known songs

"Memphis" and

"Strike like Lightening"

He really was a pretty good

Guitar player

Fast, furious and loud

My new acquaintance

Thought it was OK

I had done my duty

Lonnie finished his set

Stepped up to the mike

Thanked the audience

And said,

"Now, I like to invite a couple

Of friends to join me.

Please welcome

Keith Richards and

Ronnie Wood of

The Rolling Stones!"

Up they went

All smiles

Picked up guitars

And pitched in to

"Lonley Man" and

"Things I Used To Do"

With Lonnie

My companion was

Overcome

With admiration

At my inside knowledge

Of the underground

New York music scene

He went to the loo

And came back

To report

That Mick Jagger

Was at the urinal next to him

And he had got

Mick's autograph

Just then I looked back

And saw that

Bob Dylan was sitting

At the table in back of us

I later read that

Paul Simon was there too

But I didn't see him

And he made no effort

To seek me out

I was the recipient

Of many profuse thanks

And an autographed

Album of the musical Chess

For having shared

My secret knowledge

Of the hip music scene

With my new acquaintance

But having peaked

That night

I thought best to go out on top

And retire then

As King

Of the New York Music Scene

Manhattan: Copyright Ned Swan 2016. All rights reserved.

Made in United States
North Haven, CT
29 October 2022

26065748R00049